D1140676

Daniel Stewart's and Melville College

00009661

ANCIENT SCOTLAND

RICHARD DARGIE

Explore Scottish History is packed with historical evidence  to help you discover how Scotland's people lived in the past. It also includes links to the Heinemann Explore website and CD-ROM ⊙.

Heinemann
LIBRARY

H www.heinemann.co.uk/library
Visit our website to find out more information about Heinemann Library books.

To order:
☎ Phone 44 (0) 1865 888066
▤ Send a fax to 44 (0) 1865 314091
▭ Visit the Heinemann Library Bookshop at www.heinemann.co.uk/library to browse our catalogue and order online.

First published in Great Britain by Heinemann Library, Halley Court, Jordan Hill, Oxford OX2 8EJ, a division of Reed Educational and Professional Publishing Ltd. Heinemann is a registered trademark of Reed Educational & Professional Publishing Ltd.

OXFORD MELBOURNE AUCKLAND JOHANNESBURG BLANTYRE
GABORONE IBADAN PORTSMOUTH (NH) USA CHICAGO

© Reed Educational and Professional Publishing Ltd 2002
The moral right of the proprietor has been asserted.

All rights reserved. No part of this publication may be reproduced, stored in a retrieval system, or transmitted in any form or by any means, electronic, mechanical, photocopying, recording, or otherwise without either the prior written permission of the Publishers or a licence permitting restricted copying in the United Kingdom issued by the Copyright Licensing Agency Ltd, 90 Tottenham Court Road, London W1P 0LP.

Designed by Celia Floyd
Originated by Dot Gradations
Printed by Wing King Tong in Hong Kong

06 05 04 03 02
10 9 8 7 6 5 4 3 2 1

ISBN 0 431 14520 2 (hardback)

06 05 04 03 02
10 9 8 7 6 5 4 3 2 1

ISBN 0 431 14521 0 (paperback)

British Library Cataloguing in Publication Data

Dargie, Richard
    Ancient Scotland. – (Explore Scottish history)
    1. Scotland – History – To 1057 – Juvenile literature
    I. Title
    941.1'01

Acknowledgements

The Publishers would like to thank the following for permission to reproduce photographs:

Bridgeman Art Library (Trinity college library, Dublin) p21, Corbis p25, Hulton Getty pp18, 24, Mary Evans Picture Library pp15, 23, National Museums of Scotland pp8, 12, 17, Scotland in Focus pp4 (D Barnes), 6 (Corbett), 7 (O Burrows), 9 (D Houghton), 10 (J Byers), 11 (R Schofield), 19 (D Kerr) 20 (K Orvsdale), 22 (P Seale), 26 (R Schofield), 27, 28 (J Byers), 29 (P Turner), Scottish Cultural Resources Access Network pp13 (Archeolink), 16 (Shetland Museum), Magnet Harlequin (Terry Griffiths) p14.

Cover photograph reproduced with permission of Atlas Photography.

Our thanks to Ian Hall of the University of St Andrews for his comments during the writing of this book.

Every effort has been made to contact copyright holders of any material reproduced in this book. Any omissions will be rectified in subsequent printings if notice is given to the Publisher.

Any words appearing in the text in bold, **like this**, are explained in the glossary.

Contents

Prehistoric Scotland

Around fifteen thousand years ago, Scotland was an empty land. It was covered by a vast glacier or sheet of ice that was several hundred metres deep. In time the ice melted leaving a land of mountains, rivers and glens. **Lochans** and bogs covered much of the lower ground. Plants spread quickly and by 8000 BC, Scotland had dense forests of birch, hazel and rowan and high grassy **moorlands**. Insects, birds and animals soon followed.

The first people to arrive were **hunters** who travelled in bands of ten or twelve. At first, they moved along the coast and river **valleys** looking for shellfish or stranded seals and whales. Later, they explored Scotland's forests and moors in search of other things to gather and eat.

The first hunters were skilled people. They made tools and weapons from hard rocks such as quartz and bloodstone. They caught beasts in traps, skinned them and made shelters with the hide, stretching them over a wooden frame like a tent. In some places, like Inchnadamph in northern Scotland, they lived in caves. They lit and heated these homes using lamps made from deer bone that burned animal fat. Fire was also used to cook, and to scare away wild beasts from the shelter.

Between 7000 and 6000 BC, there were probably only around five or six hundred people living in Scotland. They moved in small bands along the coasts and the edge of the forests and mountains, passing on the knowledge of their food trails from one generation to the next.

These early people moved around Scotland and never settled long in one place. Once they had gathered all the food in an area, they moved on, leaving little **evidence** of their lives behind. Most of the things they made, such as clothes, baskets and ropes, have rotted away. Only harder objects such as tools made from stone, bone and antlers have survived down to modern times. These include harpoon heads, hooks and pins. **Archaeologists** have found these in dumps called **middens** where the first people of Scotland left their rubbish.

Archaeologists call these early hunters the **Mesolithic** people. People in Scotland lived this way for over three thousand years.

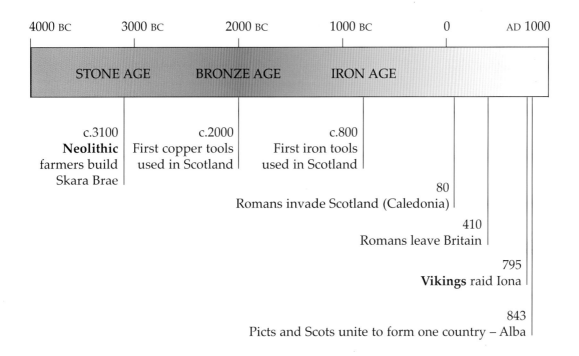

| 4000 BC | 3000 BC | 2000 BC | 1000 BC | 0 | AD 1000 |

STONE AGE   BRONZE AGE   IRON AGE

c.3100
Neolithic farmers build Skara Brae

c.2000
First copper tools used in Scotland

c.800
First iron tools used in Scotland

80
Romans invade Scotland (Caledonia)

410
Romans leave Britain

795
Vikings raid Iona

843
Picts and Scots unite to form one country – Alba

Exploring further

The Heinemann Explore CD-ROM will give you information about the ancient world. From the Contents screen you can click on the blue words to find out about Scotland and other ancient civilizations.

The mystery of Skara Brae

In 1850 a great gale ripped across the Orkney Islands off the north coast of Scotland. The winds blew away the sand dunes at a place called Skara Brae. This revealed an ancient buried village that was almost five thousand years old.

Everything at Skara Brae was made of stone. There were eight underground houses with walls of thick slabs. These had shelves and cupboards built into them. There were seats, a dresser and even box beds made of stone. The cooking hearth in the middle of each house was lined with stone. There were even stone water tanks set into the ground.

From a modern archaeologist

"Skara Brae is the most perfectly preserved Neolithic village in all of Europe. The people of Skara Brae had farming skills to add to the older ways of hunting and food-gathering. The **evidence** shows they lived well-fed lives in their warm and comfortable village."

There were many **middens** at Skara Brae. The villager's rubbish held many clues about their way of life. **Archaeologists** found thousands of bones from cattle, sheep and pigs. They also found whalebone tools for grinding corn. This meant that the Skara Brae people grew crops and herded animals. They were farmers who settled in one place. Archaeologists think that people lived and farmed at Skara Brae for over six hundred years. They call these early farmers **Neolithic**.

Archaeologists **excavated** Skara Brae in the 1920s. They realized that the ancient people left their homes in a great hurry and never went back. They left cooking pots, tools and precious ochre dye used for painting designs on **standing stones**. One pot held the last meal cooked in the village, thousands of years before. Pieces of a bead necklace lay scattered on the floor. Archaeologists think that a woman dropped it as she ran from her house in terror. It seems that perhaps the Skara Brae people had to flee when a sudden storm buried their houses under tons of sand.

Near Skara Brae is the great **burial mound** of Maes Howe. Neolithic farmers built it around 2700 BC. We think they placed the bones of their dead in it, and left offerings to their ancestors. The builders of Maes Howe were good at maths and astronomy. They built the giant tomb so that the entry passage points to the midwinter sun. On the shortest day of the year, the sun's rays shine straight into the inner chamber.

Skara Brae houses had stone beds (left) stone dressers for holding food (centre) and stone sinks in the ground for holding fresh water.

Exploring further – Ancient Egypt

Skara Brae was probably used before 2500 BC. At this time ancient Egypt was becoming powerful. Follow this path on the CD-ROM to find out about the ancient Egyptians: Exploring the Wider World > Focus On: Ancient Egypt.

People of the magic metals

The first **hunters** and farmers in Scotland used tools made from the hard stones they found. Around 2000 BC however, people in Scotland learned how to make things from metal. They discovered that some rocks contained metal **ore**. They heated the ore so that it melted and turned to liquid. Then it was poured into a mould and shaped into knives, axe heads, swords, farming tools and even jewellery.

The new metal tools and weapons were harder and sharper than the old stone ones. Warriors with metal weapons were stronger in battle. Farmers with metal axes could clear the forest more easily to open up more land for farming. The skill of metal-making must have seemed like magic to these early people.

The metal tools brought many changes to their way of life. The first metal tools were made of copper that was mined in Scotland. In time, the metal-makers learned that copper and tin mixed together made a harder metal called bronze. However there was no tin in Scotland. The nearest tin mines were in Cornwall in the south of England. So prehistoric people in Scotland had to learn to **trade** with other people in distant lands.

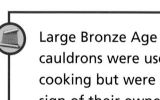 Large Bronze Age cauldrons were used for cooking but were also a sign of their owner's wealth. This cauldron was discovered in Flanders Moss in Perthshire in almost perfect condition.

Archaeologists have learned about the metal-making peoples from the **evidence** in their graves. Some tribes buried their dead in stone boxes called cists with clay pots of food and drink by their side. Perhaps these were offerings to their gods or supplies for a journey after death. After 1500 BC tribes in the north east of Scotland burned their dead and put the ashes in small clay urns called beakers. These metal-making people are called Bronze Age people.

The Bronze Age people built many impressive monuments in Scotland. The Ring of Brodgar had over 60 **standing stones**, forming a great open temple. At Cairnpapple Hill in West Lothian, they built a huge chambered **cairn** to bury their leaders.

 Ancient monuments like the Ring of Brodgar or the stone henge at Callanish may have been gigantic star clocks to help the **Neolithic** farmers know when to sow their seed or harvest their crops.

After 800 BC people in Scotland used iron. Iron ore was plentiful in Scotland and was tougher than bronze. Archaeologists think that a few people from Europe brought the skills of iron-making to Scotland and that the local people quickly copied them. They needed the new metal, for life in Scotland was becoming more troubled.

Exploring further – Ancient Greece

Around the time that iron began to be used to make tools in Scotland, the city-states of ancient Greece were being founded. The first Olympic Games we know about were held in 776BC. Discover more about the ancient Greeks on the CD-ROM: Exploring the Wider World > Focus On: Ancient Greece.

The Celts

The Celts were a skilled and well-armed people who spread across northern Europe and Britain after 800 BC. **Archaeologists** can not tell how many Celts came to Scotland during the Iron Age. However we know that by around 500 BC most people followed a Celtic way of life.

Celtic tribes lived in strong places that were easy to defend. The weather in Iron Age Scotland was cold and wet. The crop harvests were poor and many of the old Bronze Age farms were slowly covered in **peatbog**. Good farming land became scarce. We think the Celts had to fight to defend their farms from enemies.

Some Celtic tribes lived in hill-forts. They built thick walls of earth and stone around a hilltop. They strengthened these walls by digging ditches and raising a high timber **stockade**. Sometimes the Celts lived in villages lower down and only used the hill-fort in times of trouble. At Eildon Hill however, they built a vast fort that was large enough to house three thousand people.

 Some Celtic families protected themselves by building crannogs. These were houses on stilts in the middle of lochs or marshes. Wooden poles and stones were used to make an artificial island. The crannog could only be reached by boat or by a rope bridge that was cut in times of trouble.

There were many brochs across Iron Age Scotland like Mousa Broch, which still stands today, in Shetland.

The Celts also built brochs. These were high round towers made of thick stone slabs. Brochs were usually built close to farmland next to the coast. Few of them had a well, so archaeologists don't think they were lived in for long periods of time. They were probably used to protect valuable things like cattle and stores of grain from enemy raids.

Most Celtic houses were round with a timber frame and thatched roof. The walls were made of woven sticks or wicker. Mud and straw were smeared on the wicker to seal it against the wind and rain. Celtic houses often had an underground stone chamber used for keeping food stores safe from mice and rats.

 A Greek writer describes the Celts

"The Celtic nobles shave their faces but grow moustaches which cover their mouth. They do not sit on benches in their homes but sit upon wolf skins on the ground."

Exploring further – The Celts

The Digging Deeper section of the CD-ROM allows you to find out more about the topics that interest you: Digging Deeper > The Celts, gives details about Celtic life.

The Empire invades

The Romans were the most powerful people in the ancient world. Their vast **Empire** stretched across Europe and North Africa. In AD 43 the Romans invaded southern Britain. They believed that Britain was rich in valuable metals such as gold and tin. The Roman Emperor Claudius also knew that a successful war against the Celts would make him more popular with his own people. Over the next 35 years the Roman **legions** conquered the Celtic tribes in southern Britain. By AD 80 they were ready to march into the mountainous north of Britain, an area that they called Caledonia and we now call Scotland.

Agricola was the Roman general in charge of the invasion of Caledonia. His troops quickly captured the Celtic **fortress** on Eildon Hill and built a huge camp at nearby Trimontium. Agricola then used Trimontium as a base to control southern Scotland, building a chain of strong forts linked by fast, straight roads. Some southern tribes such as the Votadini in East Lothian made peace with Agricola when they saw the power of his well-armed **legionaries**. However most of the Caledonians refused to obey the Roman commander.

In AD 84 Agricola's legions marched north to crush these remaining tribes. A great horde of Celtic warriors gathered near a hill known as Mons Graupius. The Roman writer Tacitus said they were led by a chieftain called Calgacus. The two armies met in a fierce battle but the Caledonians were no match for the well-trained Roman troops. Tacitus witnessed the battle and said that the Romans lost only 360 men while the Caledonians had thousands of dead and wounded.

Many Roman helmets have been excavated at the legionary camp of Trimontium near modern day Melrose.

The Romans thought they had conquered Caledonia but the tribes did not surrender. They disappeared into the rough hill country in the north where the Romans could not follow them. In the years after the battle at Mons Graupius, the Caledonians recovered their strength and attacked the enemy forts on their land. They may even have destroyed an entire Roman legion. The Ninth Hispana Legion disappeared suddenly around the year AD 105. Some historians think the Caledonians lured their enemy into a trap near the River Solway and massacred over six thousand Roman troops. The Romans realized that Caledonia would never be part of their Empire.

The shapely hill of Bennachie may have been the site of the Battle of Mons Graupius in AD 84.

Calgacus' speech to his warriors before the battle of Mons Graupius, according to the Roman Tacitus

"We, the most distant dwellers upon the earth, the last of the free...there are no more nations beyond us, nothing but waves and rocks and the Romans who are more deadly even than these...the Romans call robbery and murder by the lying name of 'government'; they create a wilderness and call it peace."

Exploring further – Boudicca's revolt

The Celtic tribes of southern Britain also fought against the Romans. Discover more about the revolt of Boudicca on the CD-ROM. Follow this path: Exploring the Wider World > Focus On: Romans, Anglo-Saxons and Vikings > Boudicca's revolt.

The Roman walls

In AD 121 Hadrian was Emperor of Rome. He wanted to make southern Britain safe from attack by the Celtic peoples of the north – the Caledonians. He ordered his army to build a stone wall right across the island. His engineers built an impressive stone and timber wall for over 72 miles from the river Tyne to the Solway.

Hadrian's Wall was over five metres high and three metres wide. A steep ditch protected it on the northern, Caledonian side. There were sixteen large forts with space in each fort for around a thousand **legionaries**. There were gates through the wall at mile intervals. Each gate was defended by a **milecastle** manned by about 30 soldiers.

The next Emperor, Antoninus, decided to build a second wall across Caledonia. The Antonine Wall ran for 38 miles between the rivers Forth and the Clyde. It was made of turf blocks and earth with a high fence of sharp wooden stakes along the top. Near each fort, there were high platforms with iron fire beacons, used to send signals if the Caledonians attacked.

The soldiers who patrolled the Antonine Wall came from all over the Empire. Their life was tough. They had to patrol the wall, watching out for raids by Caledonian warbands. Sometimes they marched northwards into the dangerous tribal homelands to put down any trouble.

 A Roman writer describes Hadrian's Wall

"The Emperor Hadrian came to Britain in the year 122 and was the first to build a wall, over 70 miles long from sea to sea, to divide the Caledonians from the Romans."

When the wall was quiet, the soldier's life was dull but comfortable. The army provided them with good rations of wheat, which the men cooked as bread, porridge and pasta. Roman farms and orchards in southern Britain supplied the men with fresh ham, beef, fruit and vegetables. The troops also hunted deer, hare, wild fowl and **boar**. Merchants sometimes came to the wall, selling spices, honey and oil.

Antoninus's defences were meant to protect the friendly Celtic tribes in southern Caledonia who were happy with Roman rule. However after 30 years the Roman army decided to abandon the Antonine Wall. Around AD 170 it retreated to Hadrian's stronger frontier to the south. Some historians think the Romans were beaten back by Caledonian attacks. Others believe that they retreated because southern Caledonia was at peace and fewer troops were needed to patrol there.

Hadrian was born in AD 76, in Spain, but became one of the greatest of Rome's Emperors.

A Roman writer describes the building of the Antonine Wall

"The Emperor Antoninus conquered the northern Britons and after driving them back, he built a second wall, this time made of turf."

Exploring further – Hadrian's Wall

The CD-ROM carries lots of pictures showing what remains of Hadrian's Wall. These remains show us what life was like on the Wall. To see them, follow this path: Pictures > Invasion and Warfare. Click on one of the pictures to make it bigger. A caption will tell you what the picture shows.

Romans and Caledonians

Roman troops patrolled and protected southern Caledonia for over three hundred years. At first the Romans were invaders and seen as enemies by the Celtic peoples of Caledonia. In time, Romans and Caledonians mixed together and learned from each other.

Many Celtic villages and townships grew up near Roman forts and the two great walls. Instead of fighting the Romans, the local people **traded** with them. Some tribes set up farms so they could sell cattle and grain to the **legions**. One local trader opened a pottery kiln at Bearsden near Glasgow making pots and jugs for the soldiers. There were special market places across southern Caledonia where Roman traders bought leather hides, wool and timber from the Celts. Roman ships sailed from the Tay and the Forth carrying these goods to Europe.

Archaeologists can use **evidence** like these coins to work out which tribes traded with the Romans.

Sometimes the Romans took Caledonian wives. Their sons became Roman soldiers in their turn. By AD 200 many of the Roman troops on Hadrian's Wall were half-Celtic. Some friendly tribes in southern Caledonia learned to speak Latin, the language of Rome. They began to wear Roman clothes and to live like Romans. They were happy to help the Romans to keep the peace. **Archaeologists** found a great treasure of gold and silver goblets at the Votadini hill-fort of Traprain Law near Edinburgh. They think it was a gift or a bribe from the Romans to the tribesfolk so they would remain loyal to Rome.

As Romans and Caledonians mixed together more, they began to share ideas and beliefs. Brigantia was a goddess worshipped by both Celts and Romans.

Not all Caledonian tribes wanted to become Romans. By AD 300 the Caledonian tribes in the north of Scotland had united into one nation. The Romans called this new enemy 'picti' or the Picts. In AD 367 a great Pictish army smashed through Hadrian's Wall and raided deep into the southern half of the island. This was a sign that Roman power in Britain was coming to an end.

By AD 400 the Roman Empire was under attack from many new enemies. The Roman troops in Britain were needed to defend the heart of the Empire in Italy. In AD 410 all Roman troops in Britain were transferred to other parts of Europe, leaving Britain and Caledonia far behind.

A Roman writer in southern Britain in AD 410

"The barbarians drive us into the sea. The sea drives us to the barbarians. Between these two kinds of death, we are slaughtered or drowned."

Exploring further – Life in Roman Britain

To investigate daily life in Roman Britain, follow this path on the CD-ROM: Exploring the Wider World > Focus On: Romans, Anglo-Saxons and Vikings

To explore a town in Roman Britain click on: The town of Calleva.

The Picts

The Picts lived in the north and east of Scotland between AD 200 and 900. They were a Celtic people who lived in tribes led by chieftains and kings. The Picts were farmers but they had skilled craftsmen who made iron tools and weapons, and jewellery from gold and silver. They also cut giant stone slabs and covered these with carvings showing hunting and battle scenes. **Archaeologists** have found twenty-nine stone slabs with a Pictish writing called ogham. The Pictish alphabet has recently been **deciphered** so we can now read the messages on these stones.

Picti

In AD 297 a Roman writer described these northern tribes as 'picti'. Historians used to think this meant they painted their faces and bodies with war paint. However nowadays we think the name Pict comes from an ancient word 'pett' meaning a piece of land.

Like other Celtic peoples, the Picts believed in water gods. The Pictish **fortress** at Burghead in Moray contains a vast underground water well. Historians believe that the Picts drowned important prisoners here as a **sacrifice** to their gods. After AD 650 many of the Pictish tribes became Christian and gave up their old beliefs. Early Christian writers said that the Picts had special priests or wizards with magical powers.

In AD 685 the Pictish lands were invaded by the Northumbrians, a fierce people from the north of England. The Pictish king Bridei crushed the invaders at the Battle of Nechtansmere near Forfar.

 The story of the Battle of Nechtansmere was carved on the Aberlemno Stone and set up near the battlefield as a reminder of the Pictish victory.

 A description of the Battle of Nechtansmere in AD 685

"The Picts pretended to retreat and lured the Northumbrians into a narrow mountain pass. There, the Northumbrian king Egfrith was killed along with most of his army."

"There came foul hordes of Picts like worms that wriggle out of cracks in the rocks, greedy for bloodshed with evil faces covered in hair..."

A southern British writer describes Pictish warriors

In AD 700 the Picts were the strongest people in northern Britain. Yet by AD 900 their kingdoms had completely disappeared. In AD 843 the Picts united with another people, the Scots, under the Scottish king Kenneth MacAlpin. We think they did this for protection. The Pictish lands were under constant attack from the **Vikings** and they needed help. Within a few years, the Picts merged into the new Scottish kingdom. Almost all traces of their history and of their language vanished.

 ## Exploring further – Key people

The Biographies section of the CD-ROM will tell you more about famous people from ancient Scotland, like the Pictish king Bridei and Kenneth MacAlpin. You can also find out about Romans like Hadrian. Click on their names to read about these people.

A Christian land

The early Celtic tribes and the Picts were **pagan**. They worshipped many gods and spirits. The Picts thought that wells and **lochans** were holy places. Some Celtic tribes threw valuable gifts into bogs and lochs as an offering to their gods. They may even have drowned human **sacrifices** in them.

At first, the Christian faith spread slowly in Scotland. The earliest Christians in Scotland were probably Roman soldiers who lived in southern Caledonia near Hadrian's Wall.

Around AD 400 a small band of Christian **missionaries** arrived in southern Scotland from Ireland. They included St Ninian, the first known Christian in Scotland's history. Historians think he may have studied as a priest in Rome and France. Ninian and his followers built a small church at Whithorn in Galloway, the first Christian church in Scotland. Many of the oldest Christian carvings have been found here such as Peter's Cross.

The greatest Christian missionary to Scotland was Columcille or St Columba. He came from a noble family in Ireland but fled from his homeland after a **civil war** there. Columba landed on the small island of Iona where he founded a monastery in AD 563. Columba made several long, dangerous journeys to the lands of the Picts and tried to convert them to the Christian faith.

 The change to Christianity took many years. Pagan and Christian symbols appeared on the same stone carving.

Many of the first Christian missionaries to Scotland came from Ireland. Columba was followed by St Mungo and St Maelrubha who were priests in the Celtic Church. They carried the Christian message to the Picts.

Celtic priests lived alone as **hermits** in small beehive cells. Some of these survive today on islands off the west coast of Mull. Celtic priests and monks were very holy men. When they died their bones were kept as relics. The relics of St Columba were placed in a jewelled box called the Brecbannoch. For centuries, people believed Columba's relics had magic powers.

There were many Celtic monasteries in Scotland between AD 600 and 800. The richest was at Iona. Here the monks made beautiful Bibles decorated with Celtic drawings and designs.

 The most famous of the Iona Bibles is the Book of Kells which survives today in Ireland.

Exploring further – Christianity

Around the same time that Christianity first came to Scotland, it was spreading across Europe. On the CD-ROM you can read about how the new religion affected other countries. Follow this path: Exploring the Wider World > Focus On: Romans, Anglo-Saxons and Vikings > Saxon Britain: a part of Europe.

The birth of the Scottish nation

Between AD 500 and 850 there were several different peoples and kingdoms in the land we now call Scotland. Very few books and written records have survived from that time. As a result, historians sometimes call these years the Dark Ages.

The most powerful people in Dark Age Scotland were the Picts. They lived in the north and east of Scotland. The Picts were probably the **descendants** of the earlier Bronze and Iron Age peoples who had settled in Scotland.

Three peoples fought over the land in central and southern Scotland. After AD 500 the original Celtic tribes like the Votadini were sometimes called 'the British' by writers of the time. Din Eidyn or Edinburgh was the capital of the British kingdom of Gododdin. Galloway in the south west was another important British kingdom. We think the British tribes spoke a language that was like modern Welsh.

Alcluith, the fort on Dumbarton Rock, was the centre of a small kingdom called Strathclyde. Alcluith meant 'Fortress of the Britons'.

After AD 600 the British were slowly pushed out of much of their lands by newcomers from the south. Originally from Denmark, the Angles of Northumbria built a powerful kingdom in northern England. By AD 640 the Northumbrians had captured Gododdin and much of southern Scotland.

The Scots lived in Argyll and the islands off Scotland's west coast. They were a Christian people who spoke Gaelic like the people of Ireland. By AD 550 they had built an important **fortress** at Dunadd in mid-Argyll. They gradually pushed further into the mainland, capturing land from the Picts and the British.

Scotii

The Scots called their kingdom Dalriada but their enemies called them 'scotii' or raiders. In time, their kingdom became known as Scotia or land of the Scots.

In the 790s another new people came to northern Britain – the **Norse** or **Viking** invaders from Scandinavia. The Scots and Picts had to join together to fight this dangerous new enemy. In AD 843 Kenneth MacAlpin became the first king of a united Scotland. The Scots had to battle for hundreds of years to win back the land taken by the Norse and the Angles.

KENETH I.

Kenneth MacAlpin was the first king of both the Scots and the Picts. He possibly became 'King of the Picts' when their leaders were wiped out by Viking invaders.

Exploring further – Anglo-Saxon kingdoms

At this time, raiders from Europe had invaded and settled in southern Britain. You can learn about these Anglo-Saxon kingdoms on the CD-ROM: Exploring the Wider World > Focus On: Romans, Anglo-Saxons and Vikings > Anglo-Saxon raiders.

The fury from the north

In AD 795 **Norse** raiders or **Vikings** attacked the rich abbey on the island of Iona. They **plundered** the treasures of the abbey and carried the people off as slaves. There were soon many more Viking raids along the coasts of Scotland. The Norse Vikings were helped by their superb longships. These light, narrow, wooden boats could sail close to Scotland's rocky shores and far along its shallow rivers. They were also light enough to be carried overland. It seemed that the Norse could attack anywhere.

From a Norse poem describing a Viking raid:

"On Lewis Isle the fearful blaze
A house-destroying fire is raised
South of Kintyre the people fled
Scared by our swords, dyed blood red"

Most of the Vikings that came to Scotland were from Norway. At first they were just much-feared raiders in search of plunder and slaves. After AD 830 however, they began to settle in the north and west of Scotland with their families. They took over most of the islands such as the Hebrides and the Orkneys. They invaded the very north of Scotland, which they called Sutherland because it lay to the south of their homeland in Norway.

The Christian peoples of Scotland feared the Vikings. This was partly because they were strong, cunning warriors who did not seem to fear death. It was also because the Norse were different from the peoples of northern Europe. They were **pagans** who worshipped the old fierce gods.

Christian monks, who hated the Norse and exaggerated their fierceness, wrote the only histories that have survived from that time. As a result, historians used to think the Vikings slaughtered all the people in the lands they invaded. However, they were not just raiders but skilled farmers, merchants and craftsmen. **Archaeologists** now think that the Norse found an empty land when they arrived in northern Scotland. **Plague** had already wiped out many of the Picts there.

A prayer written by a monk at Lindisfarne monastery:

"Never has there been such a terror as this pagan race. From the fury of the Norsemen, deliver us O Lord."

The most important Norse lands in Scotland were the Orkney islands. After 860, they were ruled by a Norse Jarl or Earl. The Norse Jarls of Orkney were as powerful as the kings of Scotland. Thorfinn, the greatest Jarl, commanded a great fleet and army and was the friend of kings across Europe.

The promise of adventure and plunder overseas was enough to make the Vikings brave the stormy waters of the North Sea.

Exploring further – What do we know about the Vikings?

Much of what we know about the Vikings comes from the people they attacked, who hated and feared them. Follow this path to read a poem that tells us a bit about how the Vikings viewed themselves:

Written Sources > The Viking view of life.

Life in Viking Scotland

The **Vikings** settled in parts of Scotland that were like their homeland in Scandinavia. Northern Scotland was mountainous with sea lochs that cut into the coast. In Viking times Scotland's climate was warmer and drier than it is today, so the **Norse** could grow good crops and raise cattle.

Archaeologists have discovered a well-preserved Norse village at Jarlshof in Shetland.

The largest building in a Norse village was the long-hall. This is where they would gather to feast and drink during the long winter nights. There were several farm buildings and workshops where iron weapons and tools were made and repaired. Norse villages were usually built close to the sea. This was so they could easily build and repair their ships.

Although their houses were made of rough stone, turf and thatch, they were warm and comfortable inside. Animal skins and woollen hangings were used to make the houses warmer and windproof. **Archaeologists** have found many objects which tell us that the Norse were wealthy and liked luxury. A great Viking treasure hoard was found buried at Skail in Orkney. It included ornaments, jewellery, brooches and pins made of amber, gold and bronze.

The Norse often buried their treasure to keep it safe. Many of these hoards have been found by archaeologists.

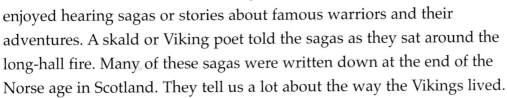

Many Norse women wore linen pinafores held up by two bronze oval brooches. Hundreds of these have been found in Viking graves around the coast of Scotland.

The Norse played games of skill such as chess. We know this because a Viking chess set was found on Lewis in the Hebrides. At their winter feasts, they enjoyed hearing sagas or stories about famous warriors and their adventures. A skald or Viking poet told the sagas as they sat around the long-hall fire. Many of these sagas were written down at the end of the Norse age in Scotland. They tell us a lot about the way the Vikings lived.

In time the Norse in Scotland became Christian. They mixed with the Scots and lost contact with their homeland in Scandinavia. Slowly the Norse lands became part of the Scottish kingdom. In 1472 Orkney and Shetland became part of Scotland. The Viking age was over after almost seven hundred years.

Norse words in Scottish placenames:

Kirkwall	kirkja – a church
Lerwick	vik or wik – a sheltered bay or harbour
Ullapool	boll or pool – a farm
Dingwall	ting – meeting place

Exploring further – The Viking way of life

The Digging Deeper section of the CD-ROM contains lots of information about the Vikings. Follow this path:

Digging Deeper > The Vikings.

The kings of Alba

By AD 900 much of modern Scotland lay within a kingdom known as Alba. Each district of this kingdom was governed by a Mormaer, or Earl. He protected the local people in return for their loyalty. The Mormaers helped to crown the king of Alba on the Stone of Destiny at Scone.

 The replica of the Stone of Destiny stands outside Scone Palace where the Kings of the Scots were crowned.

Between AD 900 and 1050 the people of Alba were lucky to have strong kings who led them in wars against their enemies. The greatest of the Alban kings was Constantine II who **reigned** for over 40 years. He weakened the power of the **Norse** and the Angles and won back land from them. Under Constantine, Alba became the strongest kingdom in northern Britain.

 Written by a modern historian

"Constantine and the other Alban kings were the true founders of the Scottish nation."

"Most Scottish kings died young in battle. Constantine II was so successful that he lived to die peacefully in his old age."

The country we know as Scotland began to take shape under the Alban kings. The capital moved from distant Argyll into the centre of Scotland in Perthshire. From here, the king could visit all parts of the country more easily. The key **fortress** of Edinburgh was also captured from the Angles in 962.

In 1018 Malcolm II of Alba led a great army south into England. Malcolm met and defeated the Anglian army at a village called Carham on the river Tweed. As a result of this victory, he won back the Lothians and the Border lands. The Tweed has marked the boundary between Scotland and England ever since. The King of Alba now ruled almost all the land in northern Britain except for the Norselands in the far north and west.

By the end of the first millenium, the peoples of northern Britain had begun to unite under one king and one flag. Alba or Scotland was a Christian kingdom with many churches and abbeys. Most people spoke Gaelic but Norn, the language of the Norse, was heard in the Viking north. The ancient tongue of the Picts was dying out but a new language called Inglis was spoken by some who lived in southern Scotland.

By AD 1000 Scotland was changing. The early Scots had many links to Ireland but these slowly faded over time. Scottish kings now looked to England and Europe for new ideas. Old places such as Iona and Dunadd, which were settled by the early Scots, lost their importance. They were replaced by new towns like Dunfermline and Edinburgh. A new Kingdom of the Scots was taking shape.

 By AD 1000 Din Eidyn or Edinburgh was an important fortress on Alba's southern border with Northumbria.

 ## Exploring further – Searching the ancient world

To find more information about the ancient world click on Search on the top panel of the Contents page. Pick a word from the keywords on the next page and click on Enter. The screen will now show a list of pages on the CD-ROM that mention this word. Click on the names of the pages to find out what they show.

Timeline

15,000 BC	Ice Age in Scotland
12,000	Ice sheets start to retreat from Scotland
8000	Scotland becomes densely forested
7000	First **hunting** people arrive in Scotland
3100	**Neolithic** farmers build village of Skara Brae
2500	Skara Brae abandoned, possibly because of fierce storm
2000	First copper tools are used in Scotland
800	First iron tools are used in Scotland
200	Brochs start to be built in Scotland
AD 43	Romans invade Britain
80	Romans start invasion of Caledonia
121–127	Hadrian builds a wall to protect England from the Picts
367	Picts break though Hadrian's Wall and attack England
410	Romans leave Britain
793	**Vikings** invade Iona and sack abbey
800	Viking attacks on Pictland get well under way
830	**Norse** settle in Orkney and Shetland
843	Picts and Scots unite to become one country known as Alba. Kenneth MacAlpin becomes king.
850	Norse settle in Ross, Sutherland and Caithness
903–943	**Reign** of King Constantine II
1042–1057	Reign of Macbeth, one of the last Alban kings

Glossary

archaeologist scientist who finds and examines evidence from the past

boar fierce wild pigs with tusks that live in forests

burial mound large earth-covered chamber used for burying the dead

cairn pile of stones raised over a grave to form a roof

civil war war in which both sides are from the same people or country

decipher crack the meaning of a code or an unknown alphabet

descendants offspring such as children and grandchildren

empire large kingdom ruled by a powerful monarch or Emperor

evidence facts and objects used to discover the truth about the past

excavate dig carefully into an ancient site looking for evidence

fortress strong place of safety and defence usually made of stone

hermit monk who is shut away from other people and the world

hunter someone who catches their food by trapping and killing it

legion regiment in the Roman army, usually around 6000 men

legionaries fulltime infantry or foot-soldiers in a Roman legion

lochan small loch or lake in Scotland, often very marshy

Mesolithic Middle Stone Age which lasted from about 8000-5000 BC

middens heaps of rubbish left by ancient people

milecastle small fort on Hadrian's Wall, built at mile intervals

missionaries people who try to convert others to their faith

moorland unfarmed land, often boggy and covered in wild heath

Neolithic New Stone Age which lasted from about 5000-1000 BC

Norse people who came to Scotland from Norway after AD 800

ore mineral rock that also contains pieces of metal

pagan someone who is not Christian and worships many gods

peatbog bog covered in ancient black/brown vegetable matter

plague sickness or disease often spread by fleas or rats

plunder treasure and other goods carried off by raiders

reign rule as a king or queen

standing stones circles of large ceremonial stones found throughout northern Scotland

sacrifice killing of animals or human prisoners as a gift to the gods

stockade fence or wall made of sharply pointed wooden stakes

trade selling or exchange of goods by merchants

valley flatter ground between hills, often watered by a river

Vikings name traditionally given to Norse raiders from Scandinavia

Index

Titles in the *Explore Scottish History* series include:

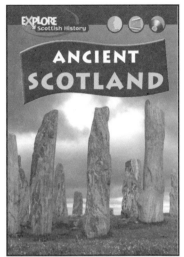

Hardback   0 431 14520 2

Hardback   0 431 14522 9

Hardback   0 431 14524 5

Hardback   0 431 14526 1

Hardback   0 431 14530 x

Find out about the other titles in this series on our website www.heinemann.co.uk/library